IT'S A FACT!

Real-Life Reads

MEGALODON
Prehistoric Predator of the Deep

by Ruth Owen

Consultants:

Suzy Gazlay, MA
Recipient, Presidential Award for Excellence in Science Teaching

Catalina Pimiento, MA, Biologist
University of Florida

Published in 2015 by Ruby Tuesday Books Ltd.

Editor: Mark J. Sachner
Designer: Emma Randall
Production: John Lingham

Photo Credits:
Alamy: 7; Corbis: 18–19, 25, 26–27; Jayson Kowinsky/www.fossilguy.
com: 13, 24; Public Domain: 17; Ruby Tuesday Books: 4–5, 8–9, 20;
Shutterstock: Cover, 10–11, 12, 14–15, 21, 28–29, 31; Superstock:
Cover, 16, 22–23.

Library of Congress Control Number: 2013920129

ISBN 978-1-909673-60-1

Printed and published in the United States of America

For further information including rights and permissions requests, please
contact our Customer Service Department at 877-337-8577.

CONTENTS

Terror from Below!

A whale slowly swims in the ocean. It rises to the water's surface to breathe. The huge creature does not know it is about to take its last breath.

From deep below the whale, an attack is coming. A giant hunter, the size of a bus, speeds upward through the water. With a single bite, the hunter tears off one of the whale's fins. Now the terrified whale cannot swim. It can only wait for the next terrible bite and then death.

The whale's giant attacker is a shark. It is the largest, most powerful shark that ever lived.

Megalodon!

Megalodon was a gigantic prehistoric shark. It lived and hunted in oceans all over the world.

Megalodon was not the only type of prehistoric shark. There have been sharks on Earth for more than 400 million years. No other type of shark has ever grown as large as Megalodon, though.

Megalodon first appeared on Earth about 16 million years ago. It died out about 2 million years ago. So if Megalodon is **extinct**, how do we know this enormous **predator** ever existed?

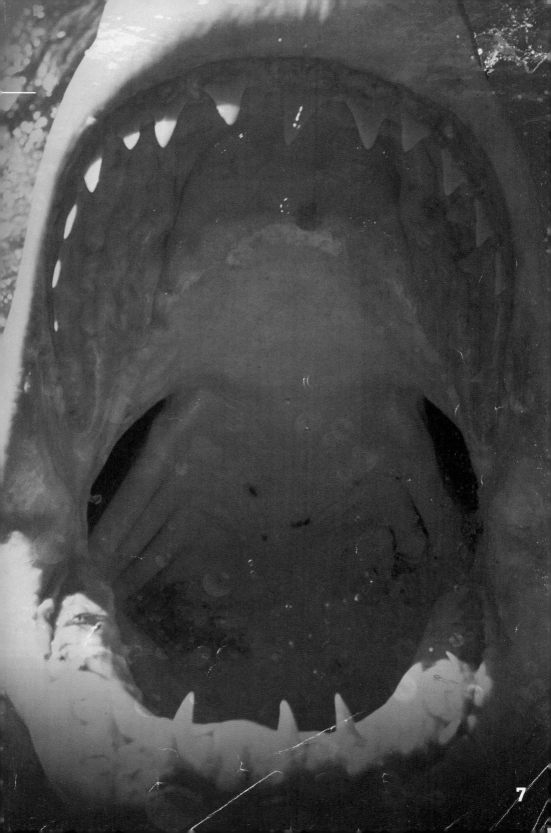

We know that prehistoric animals and plants existed because of **fossils**. So how did these rocky clues form?

Many fossils formed in seas and lakes. When an animal died, the soft, fleshy parts of its body rotted away. Soon, all that was left were hard bones and teeth.

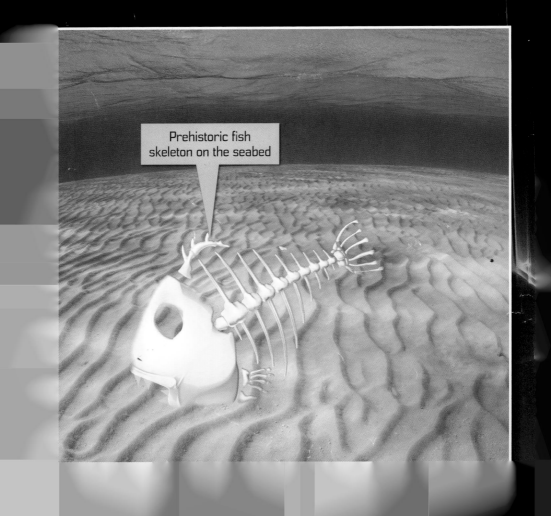

Prehistoric fish skeleton on the seabed

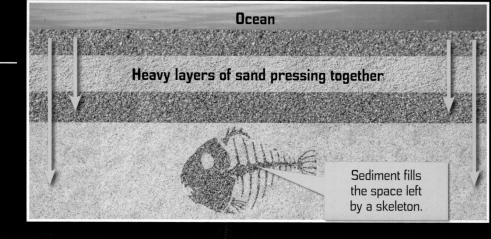

Ocean

Heavy layers of sand pressing together

Sediment fills the space left by a skeleton.

The animal's skeleton became covered with **sediment**, or sand. As the skeleton crumbled away, sediment filled the spaces left by the bones and teeth. More and more layers then settled on top. The heavy layers pressed together. Over millions of years, the sediment became rock. Inside the rock, a fossil, or rocky copy, of the animal's teeth and bones formed.

The top layers of rock are worn away by wind and rain.

A fossil inside the rock is revealed.

Today, many prehistoric seas and lakes have dried up. This makes it possible for people to find rocks that contain fossils. Some rocks even contain Megalodon fossils!

So when did people first discover Megalodon? The story is as fascinating as the creature itself!

Many hundreds of years ago, people found large, black, pointed stones in rocks. They thought these objects were the tongues of dragons that had been turned to stone.

People believed that tongue stones were magical. They thought the stones could stop the effects of poison. For example, if an enemy poisoned a person's wine, a tongue stone could be put into the drink. Then, people believed, the stone would stop the poison from working.

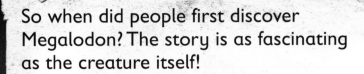

People also believed that a tongue stone could be held on a snakebite. They believed it would stop the snake's venom, or poison, from killing the victim.

A tongue stone

An Ancient Giant

In the 1600s, a scientist named Nicolaus Steno made a very important discovery.

Steno had examined many tongue stones. Then, one day, he was given the head of a freshly killed shark to cut up and study. Steno noticed that the shark's teeth looked very similar to tongue stones. The teeth were much smaller, though. Steno came to the conclusion that tongue stones must be teeth from huge sharks. He also realized that these giant sharks lived a very long time ago.

Great white shark teeth

In the 1600s, this was a brand new idea. People had found many fossils. They did not know, however, that they were the remains of ancient animals.

A fossilized Megalodon tooth embedded in rock

A Terrifying Tooth

Today we are certain that the ancient tongue stones are fossilized teeth. The giant shark that once hunted with these teeth has been named Megalodon.

Megalodon teeth have been found all over the world. They have even been found far from the sea in deserts and on mountains. That's because, millions of years ago, these places were covered by prehistoric seas.

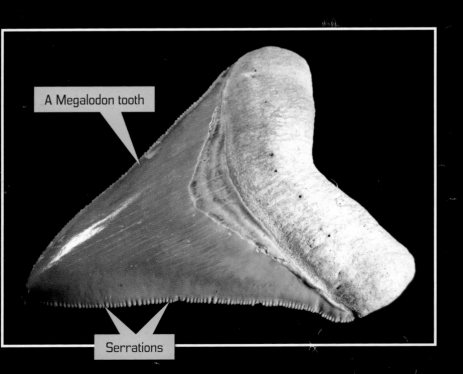

A Megalodon tooth

Serrations

Megalodon means
"big tooth" in Greek.

The largest Megalodon teeth have sides that measure
7 inches (18 cm) long. They can weigh as much as a full
can of soda. Along the edge of each tooth are hundreds
of razor-sharp points called **serrations**.

Making a Megalodon

Like all sharks, Megalodon lost teeth and grew
new ones throughout its life. Thousands of its
fossil teeth have been found.

So how big were the jaws that held these enormous
teeth? In 1909, a scientist named Bashford Dean built
a model of a Megalodon jaw. To figure out what shape
to make the model, he studied modern-day sharks.
He filled the jaw with real fossil teeth.

A great white shark

A shark's mouth is like a conveyor belt of teeth.
As the front teeth fall out, new ones are waiting to move forward.

Bashford Dean with his model Megalodon jaw at the American Museum of Natural History in New York

Today, scientists think Dean's model was a little too large and the wrong shape. It was a good start, however. Scientists were beginning to picture what Megalodon looked like.

Over the years, other scientists studied Megalodon's teeth and made model jaws.

Some scientists have estimated that Megalodon's jaws were about 7.5 feet (2.3 m) tall and 8.5 feet (2.6 m) wide. So if its jaws were so large, how big was its body?

This has been a difficult question to answer. Like all sharks, Megalodon's skeleton was made of soft, rubbery **cartilage**, not bone. When a Megalodon died, the cartilage rotted away quickly. There was not enough time for fossils to form. So scientists did not have many fossils to study and measure.

To solve the mystery, scientists studied modern-day sharks. They compared the lengths of sharks to the sizes of their jaws and teeth. Using jaw models and their measurements of Megalodon's teeth, they estimated its length.

What they discovered was truly terrifying!

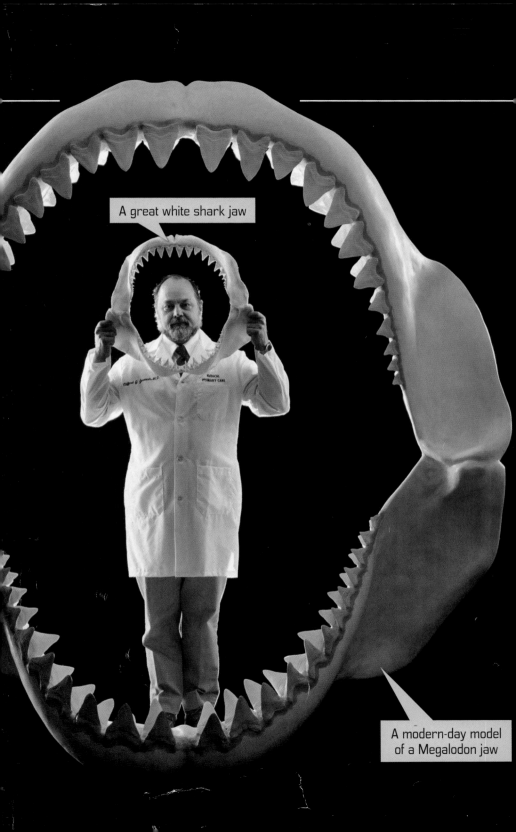

A great white shark jaw

A modern-day model of a Megalodon jaw

Imagine a creature longer than a bus with a mouth that could swallow a great white shark. That was Megalodon.

This huge shark grew to 60 feet (18.3 m) long. It probably weighed more than 100 tons (91 tonnes). That's about the same weight as 20 elephants.

No one knows for sure how Megalodon looked. Scientists think, however, that it looked similar to a great white shark. Its head was probably chunkier, though, with a blunt snout.

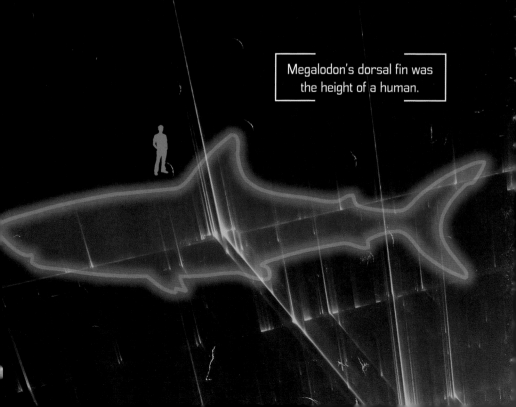

Megalodon's dorsal fin was the height of a human.

How Big Was Megalodon?

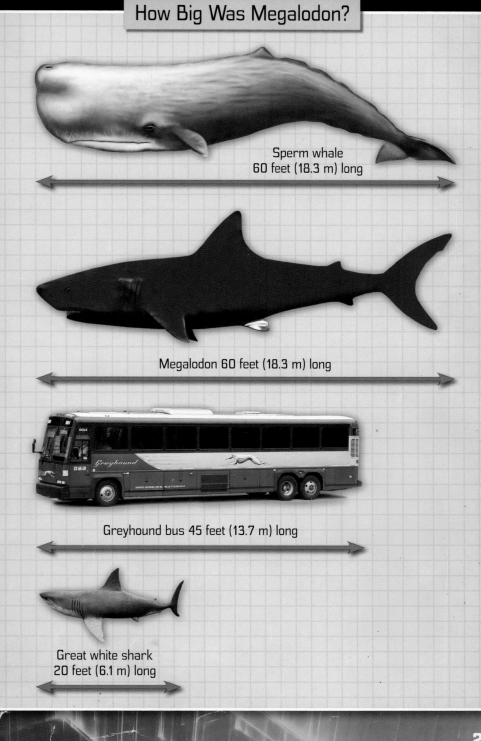

Sperm whale
60 feet (18.3 m) long

Megalodon 60 feet (18.3 m) long

Greyhound bus 45 feet (13.7 m) long

Great white shark
20 feet (6.1 m) long

A Killer Bite

Megalodon's huge jaws were able to swallow its **prey** whole.

Megalodon didn't only attack small animals, though. It also attacked prey much bigger than itself.

Megalodon's teeth were edged with jagged serrations. This shows scientists that its razor-sharp teeth were designed for tearing. Megalodon could kill large animals by tearing them into bite-sized chunks.

The force of Megalodon's bite was also deadly. Scientists have estimated that its powerful jaws could crush a car!

23

Top Predators

Megalodon was one of the top predators in the prehistoric oceans where it lived. Any other animal could become its prey.

The giant predator probably hunted prehistoric whales. Scientists know this because they have found fossil whalebones with deep gashes in them. The gashes match Megalodon's teeth. To catch a large whale, Megalodon may have bitten off the animal's tail or fin. This stopped the whale from swimming away. Then, Megalodon could take bite after bite from the dying animal.

A piece of fossilized whale backbone

Gashes from a Megalodon's teeth

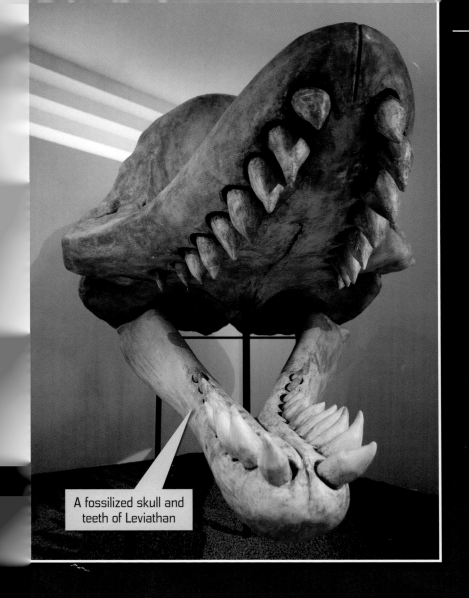

A fossilized skull and teeth of Leviathan

Megalodon was not the only giant predator around.
It shared its ocean home with a whale known as Leviathan.
This huge whale was about the same size as Megalodon.
Its teeth grew to over 12 inches (30.5 cm) long.

Extinct

For more than 14 million years, Megalodon ruled Earth's prehistoric oceans. Then the biggest shark that ever lived died out.

No one knows for sure why Megalodon became extinct. Did some of the animals that Megalodon hunted die out? If so, did it become difficult for the giant shark to find enough food? Did new types of predators appear? Did these animals eat Megalodon's prey, and even hunt Megalodon?

For now, scientists can only make guesses and keep searching for clues. The mystery of what happened to Megalodon is still to be solved!

A life-size model of a Megalodon at the Muenchehagen dinosaur park in Germany

Alive Today?

Megalodon must have been a truly incredible creature. It's not surprising, therefore, that some people hope it could still be alive today.

These people say Megalodon could be living in deep areas of ocean that have never been explored. Scientists say this is not possible. In order for Megalodon to still be alive, it would have to **breed**. This means there would need to be a large number of them. No Megalodon bodies or fresh teeth have ever been found, however.

A great white shark

Today, the largest predatory shark alive is the great white. Megalodon is gone forever.

Glossary

breed (BREED)
To mate and produce young.

cartilage (KAR-tuh-lij)
Strong, rubbery tissue that forms the skeletons of sharks and some other types of fish. In the human body, it is the tissue that forms a person's ears.

extinct (ek-STINGKT)
No longer existing.

fossils (FOSS-uhlz)
Hard, rocky copies of the remains of ancient plants and animals. Fossils form in rock over millions of years.

predator (PRED-uh-tur)
An animal that hunts and eats other animals.

prey (PRAY)
An animal that is hunted by other animals for food.

sediment (SED-uh-muhnt)
Tiny pieces of rock that have broken away from larger rocks. Pebbles and sand are both types of sediment.

serrations (ser-AY-shuhnz)
Small, pointed projections that are usually sharp and made for cutting. The edges of shark teeth have serrations.

Index

Read More

Arnold, Caroline. *Giant Shark: Megalodon, Prehistoric Super Predator.* New York: Clarion Books (2000).

Owen, Ruth. *Great White Shark (Real Life Sea Monsters).* New York: Rosen Publishing (2014).

Learn More Online

To learn more about Megalodon, go to
www.rubytuesdaybooks.com/megalodon